Political Profiles
Joe Biden

Joseph Robinette Biden Jr.

Political Profiles
Joe Biden

Jeff C. Young

PUBLISHING

Greensboro, North Carolina

Political Profiles

Joe Biden
Hillary Clinton
Al Gore
Ted Kennedy
John Lewis
John McCain
Barack Obama
Sarah Palin
Nancy Pelosi
Arnold Schwarzenegger

Political Profiles: Joe Biden

Copyright © 2010 by Morgan Reynolds Publishing

Library of Congress Cataloging-in-Publication Data

Young, Jeff C., 1948-
  Political profiles : Joe Biden / by Jeff C. Young. -- 1st ed.
     p. cm.
  Includes bibliographical references and index.
  ISBN 978-1-59935-131-5 (alk. paper)
  1. Biden, Joseph R.--Juvenile literature. 2. Vice presidents--United
States--Biography--Juvenile literature. 3. Legislators--United States--
Biography--Juvenile literature. 4. United States. Senate--Biography--
Juvenile literature. I. Title.
  E840.8.B54Y68 2009
  973.932092--dc22
  [B]
                                          2009028467

Printed in the United States of America
First Edition

To Natasha Gates, a really grand, grandniece

Contents

Vice President Joe Biden and wife Jill Biden
dance at the Eastern Inaugural Ball in Washington

Chapter *1*

Get Up!

I n his remarkable life, through successes, setbacks, and tragedies, Joe Biden has managed to stay focused and balanced because he remembers two simple words of advice his father had given him—"Get up!"

"To me this is the first principle of life, the foundational principle, and a lesson that you can't learn at the feet of any wise man: Get up!" Biden says. "The art of living is simply the act of getting up after you've been knocked down. It's a lesson taught by example and learned in the doing."

Joseph Robinette Biden Jr. was born in Scranton, Pennsylvania, on November 20, 1942. His father, Joseph Robinette Biden Sr., was an auto dealer and his mother, Catherine, a housewife. Joe was the oldest of their four children.

When Joe was ten, his family moved from Scranton to Claymont, Delaware, where Biden's life revolved around family, friends, and the Catholic Church. From all accounts, he enjoyed a pleasant childhood.

At Archmere Academy in Claymont, Delaware, Biden was a popular and athletic student. During his junior and senior years, he was the class president. In his senior year, he was the leading scorer on their undefeated football team. But, a serious speech impediment made him the butt of cruel jokes and remarks.

In his high school Latin class Joe and his classmates were taught the Latin word *impedimenta,* which means the baggage that impedes a person's progress. Joe's classmates began cruelly calling him "Joe Impedimenta" because of his speech impediment.

Joe had a pronounced stutter that would get worse in uncomfortable social situations. "It wasn't always bad," Biden recalled. "When I was at home with my brother and sister, hanging out with my neighborhood friends, or shooting the bull on the ball field, I was fine, but when I got thrown into a new situation or a new school, had to read in front of class, or wanted to ask out a girl, I just couldn't do it. My freshman year of high school, because of the stutter, I got an exemption from public speaking."

If it hadn't been for his athletic ability, the teasing and ridicule he received would have been even worse. Sports gave Joe a way to fit in and find acceptance. "As much as I lacked confidence in my ability to communicate verbally, I always had confidence in my athletic ability. Sports was as natural to me as speaking was unnatural. And sports turned out to be my ticket to acceptance and more."

Still, Joe realized that he couldn't go through life avoiding awkward situations. He also realized that his stutter stemmed from nervousness and a lack of self-confidence. Until he learned

Joe Biden is number thirty, on the top row, second from the right, in this 1961 yearbook photo.

to control it, the stutter was going to hold him back. It was time to get up and overcome that obstacle.

"I prayed that I would grow out of the stutter, but I wasn't going to leave this to chance. I was going to beat the stutter. And I went at it the only way I knew how: I worked like hell. Practice, practice, practice. I would memorize long passages of [William Butler] Yeats and [Ralph Waldo] Emerson, then stand in front of the mirror in my room on Wilson Road and talk, talk, talk."

As an additional incentive for overcoming his stutter, Joe remembered his uncle, Blewitt, who was known as Uncle "Boo-Boo." Joe's uncle was a very intelligent man and the only member of Joe's family who had a college degree. Yet, his uncle never overcame a similar stuttering problem and he blamed it for his lot in life.

"Uncle Boo-Boo had a terrible stutter his entire life, and he used it as a crutch, an excuse for everything that he didn't accomplish. He never married, never had children, and never made a home of his own. He had so much talent and he squandered it."

By his sophomore year in high school, Joe no longer had to be excused from public speaking. He was able to deliver a five-minute speech during the high school's morning assembly. When he was a senior, he was confident enough to deliver the welcoming remarks at his high school commencement. That was a personal affirmation that he had finally licked the stutter.

"I beat the stutter with a lot of hard work and with the support of my teachers and my family. But I have never really let go of my impedimenta, it's not a heavy load, but it's always with me, like a touchstone, as a reminder that everybody carries his or her own burdens—most of them a lot bigger than mine—and nobody deserves to be made smaller for having them, and nobody should be cosigned to carry them alone."

Before enrolling at the University of Delaware in 1961, Biden had pretty well decided on a career in politics. In 1960, Senator John F. Kennedy was the Democrat's presidential nominee. Like Biden, Kennedy was a Catholic. At that time, America had never elected a Catholic as its president. Many political observers believed that it never would.

Kennedy stunned those observers by narrowly defeating the Republican nominee, Vice President Richard M. Nixon. Kennedy's victory opened a vista of possibilities for Biden. Besides being the first Catholic president, Kennedy, at age forty-three, became America's youngest elected president. His election inspired Biden and many other college students in the 1960s to pursue careers in government and public service.

Opposite page: Joe Biden's senior portrait, as it appears in the Archmere Academy 1961 yearbook. Biden attended Archmere from 1957 through 1961, and served as president of the class in his junior and senior years. He was also a member of the Varsity Club.

However, Biden wasn't similarly inspired to rigorously pursue his studies. Academics took a backseat to playing football and enjoying an active social life. After taking college prep courses at Archmere Academy, Biden didn't find college to be that difficult. One of Biden's college roommates recalled: "Biden was the kind of guy who could read someone else's notes and do better on the exam than the guy who made the notes."

After Joe Biden Sr. saw his son's first semester grades, he forbade him to play spring football. Biden was still slow to change his ways. Sports, dating, and political discussions with his friends still came first. Then, as now, Biden demonstrated an engaging and glib personality. But by his junior year, he knew that if he was going to get into law school, grades and test scores would matter more than charm. "In the first semester of my junior year, I started to get a little worried. I was no longer sure, given the state of my academic transcript, that I could talk my way into a good law school."

Biden talked to David Ingersoll, who was a political science professor at the university. Ingersoll gave Biden some advice that served as a wake-up call. He told Biden that he had exactly three semesters left to improve his grades enough to impress law school admissions officials. Ingersoll added that he also needed to take extra classes all three semesters.

Biden followed Ingersoll's advice. Over the next two semesters he earned thirty-seven credit hours. (A normal load would have been thirty to thirty-two hours). While taking the extra classes, Biden brought his grades up to a B-minus grade point average.

Even while he was taking extra classes, Biden tried to make the football team as a walk-on (no athletic scholarship) player. He hadn't played for two years, but he was feeling good about his chances. After practicing hard and doing well in the annual spring game, he had steadily moved up the team's depth chart.

A spring break romance ended Biden's football plans and ultimately determined his choice of a law school. During spring break of his junior year, Biden went to Fort Lauderdale, Florida. At that time, Fort Lauderdale was a very popular spring break destination for college students. The sunny beaches were crowded with attractive and fun-loving coeds, but Biden soon became bored. Drinking was one of the primary activities for spring breakers and he didn't drink.

A couple of Biden's friends asked him to leave Florida and fly to Paradise Island in the Bahamas with them. Biden eagerly accepted the invitation even though he was low on funds. He figured that if they couldn't find free lodging there, they could head back to Fort Lauderdale.

Before they even got to the airport, Biden and his friends met some other college guys who were going to Paradise Island. They agreed to let Biden and his college friends stay in their rental house for free. With their housing problems solved, Biden and his friends headed for the beach. That's where they found themselves on the outside looking in.

A chain link fence that ran to the water's edge separated the public beach from the private beach at the British Colonial Hotel. On the other side of the fence they saw a bevy of attractive and desirable coeds working on their tans. They all decided that somehow, some way they were going to get past that fence.

"We could see dozens of beautiful young college girls sunning themselves on the British Colonial beach. . . . The three of us liberated some towels that guests had hung on the fence to dry, wrapped them around our waists so the British Colonial

Insignia was in plain sight, and walked past the guards at the main entrance. We walked like we belonged and it worked."

Once Biden got past the fence, he made a beeline for a green-eyed blonde who had caught his eye. He introduced himself to her. To Biden's delight, she responded with a warm smile. "When she turned toward me, I could see that she had a beautiful smile and gorgeous green eyes. She was lit by the unforgiving glory of a full afternoon sun, and I couldn't see a single flaw. Basically, I fell ass over tin cup in love—at first sight."

After a little bit of getting to know you chitchat, Biden learned that her name was Neilia Hunter and that she was a senior at Syracuse University. But while they were chatting, another suitor approached Neilia. His name was John and he asked Neilia if they were still going out that evening. Biden nervously awaited her answer. She politely told John that Biden was taking her to dinner. "I felt my heart go thumpa-thumpa, like it was going to go out of my chest, I mean I thought that we were just talking."

John left and Biden wanted to make sure Neilia meant what she had just said. He asked her to dinner. At that moment, Biden had $17 in his wallet. When she said yes, he asked if it would be okay to just go out for a burger. Once again, Neilia said yes.

After dinner, Biden quickly learned that island prices were a good deal higher than American prices. The tab was $20 and the waitress was looming behind Biden waiting for her money. Neilia came to his rescue.

"I could feel myself sweating . . . until I felt a tap on my knee. It was Neilia's hand and when I put my hand down to meet hers, she handed me two twenties." Biden told Neilia he was embarrassed to take her money, but she told him not to be.

For the next four days and nights Biden and Neilia were constant companions. Spring break was quickly coming to an end.

Biden wasn't going to let her get away. On day four, he more or less proposed to her. "You know we're going to get married," he told her. Neilia looked Biden in the eye and softly replied: "I think so."

The following weekend, Biden borrowed his dad's car and drove 320 miles to visit Neilia at her parent's house in Syracuse, New York. Biden found that the more he was with her, the more he wanted to stay with her. For the rest of the school year, Biden spent every weekend seeing Neilia.

During his senior year at the University of Delaware, Biden avoided taking any Friday classes. That gave him an extra day to see Neilia. He also gave up on playing football. His time outside of school was devoted to seeing her and making future plans.

"I had plenty of time to game out the future Neilia and I talked about. Graduation in a year. Law school. The wedding. The children. She wanted five and that was okay by me."

In 1965, Biden graduated from the University of Delaware with a B.A. in history and political science. Since Neilia had a teaching job in Syracuse, Biden applied to the Syracuse University College of Law. During his senior year, he had raised his grade point average and he also did well on the Law School Admissions Test. He was accepted, but he had to scramble to come up with the money to attend.

A combination of savings, financial aid, and a part-time job as resident advisor in an undergraduate dorm gave him the means to go to law school. Since academics had always come easily, Biden didn't take his first year of law school very seriously. He didn't buy all the required textbooks and his class attendance was sporadic. Biden made up for his absences by copying notes from a cooperative classmate.

His cavalier attitude toward his studies eventually caught up with him. In a technical writing class, Biden improperly cited passages from an article in the *Fordham Law Review.* Because he had been skipping the class, he didn't know how to properly do legal citations. Biden had to appear before the law school faculty and explain his error.

"The deans and the professors were satisfied that I had not intentionally cheated, but they told me I'd have to retake the course next year. . . the basic message was that I had better show some discipline or I'd never get through the first year."

Syracuse University, New York, NY

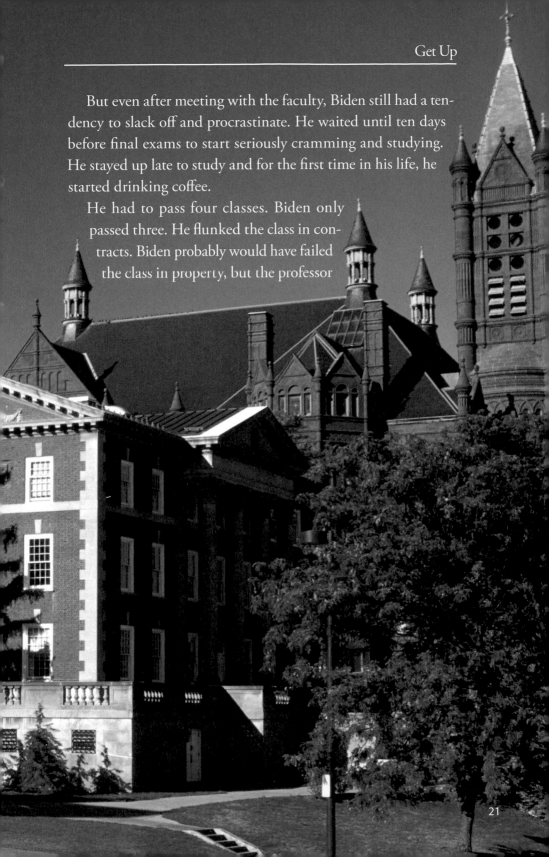

But even after meeting with the faculty, Biden still had a tendency to slack off and procrastinate. He waited until ten days before final exams to start seriously cramming and studying. He stayed up late to study and for the first time in his life, he started drinking coffee.

He had to pass four classes. Biden only passed three. He flunked the class in contracts. Biden probably would have failed the class in property, but the professor died and everyone in the class received a passing grade. In spite of his failing grade in contracts, Biden was allowed to return for his second year of law school.

On August 27, 1966, Biden married Neilia. Biden had never doubted Neilia's love, but he knew Neilia's father had some serious misgivings. At one time, he had told Neilia that she had to end the relationship because Biden was a Catholic. When she refused, he backed off. In time Biden's charm, ambition, and intelligence helped to win Neilia's father over to their side.

"His daughter was marrying a Catholic, a guy with almost no money . . . and a Democrat. But Mr. Hunter showed me in a hundred small ways that if Neilia had endless faith in me, his faith in me would match."

In 1968, Biden received his J.D. degree. His academic record was unimpressive. He graduated sixty-seventh in a class of eighty-five. But in the classes that really interested him, like legislation and international law, he got high marks. He had also shown a talent for public speaking. That was further proof that he had whipped his stuttering problem.

Thanks in part to his father, Biden landed a job with a well established firm in Wilmington, Delaware. Biden's father had a friend in the car business whose son was a superior court judge. The judge got Biden an interview with the firm of Prickett, Ward, Burt & Sanders. They offered Biden a salary of $5,200 a year and promised to bump it up to $8,000 a year when he passed the bar exam.

Now Biden was ready to embark on a new phase of his life as a husband and attorney. But he would soon find that working for a firm representing wealthy companies and corporations wasn't for him. His time at Prickett, Ward, Burt & Sanders would be short. His brief legal career would be a prelude to his real desire —a career in politics.

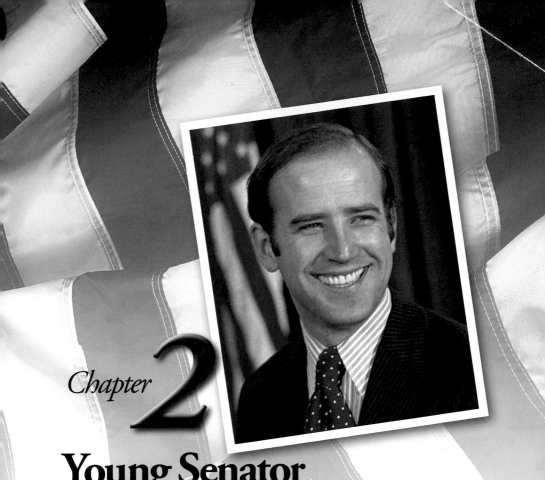

Chapter 2

Young Senator

Shortly after accepting the position with Prickett, Ward, Burt & Sanders, Biden began cramming for the Delaware bar exam. At that time, Neilia was in her first pregnancy. The $2,800 pay raise for passing the bar exam became extremely important. He passed the exam and got his raise, but he soon realized that he wasn't going to be happy working at that firm.

His misgivings first began when Prickett asked him to organize the annual Christmas party that the firm hosted for the Delaware Young Republicans. Apparently, Biden's political leanings hadn't been discussed during his job interview. Some of his co-workers at the firm mentioned that Biden should join the

Young Republicans. He demurred without telling them why. "I couldn't tell them I could never join a party that was headed by Richard Nixon or that I wasn't comfortable representing the firm's bread-and-butter clients, which were big corporations."

The clincher came when Biden watched Prickett defend a company that was being sued by one of its workers. The worker was a welder who been badly burned while on the job. Unfortunately, the welder testified that he hadn't been wearing his protective clothing. He kept it off so he could squeeze into a tight work space.

Prickett argued that the welder was negligent for not wearing the protective clothing. Biden knew that there was nothing illegal or unethical about Prickett's defense. He was simply doing his job by citing the relevant law and defending his client. Yet, Biden felt like he was on the wrong side in this case.

"The plaintiff [the person suing] had been disabled and permanently disfigured and there was a possibility that he would get nothing. I wasn't built to look the other way because the law demanded it. The law might be wrong. I felt like I should have been representing the plaintiff, that my place was with people who were outside the reach of the system."

Sometime in 1969, Biden left the firm to become a public defender. In 1964, the U.S. Supreme Court decision *Gideon v. Wainwright* mandated that a defendant couldn't go to trial without having a lawyer to defend him. If a defendant couldn't afford to hire a lawyer, then the state was legally obligated to provide him with one. Working as a public defender gave Biden ample experience in criminal law and satisfied his need for personal fulfillment.

"Being a public defender was never easy, but it was the first time that I felt like I was an actor in upholding the Constitution.

Most of the clients I drew were poor African Americans from East Wilmington, and whether they were guilty or innocent, I did my best to make sure that they were well represented at trial."

Working as a public defender was satisfying to Biden, but it wasn't paying enough to support a family. His first son, Joseph R. "Beau" Biden III, was born in 1969. The public defender position was a part-time position with a part-time salary. Biden took on a second job working for the law firm Arensen & Balick.

The firm's senior partner, Sid Balick, became a mentor attorney to Biden. He taught Biden how to keep a jury focused on the main issue or issues of a case. Balick also taught Biden how important it was to reassure clients that their attorney was genuinely concerned about them. "I learned how to be a good lawyer by watching Sid Balick. . . . Sid taught me how to help people in the toughest spots in their lives. Beyond good legal help, they needed to be reassured enough to get them past the panic. Sid showed me the importance of putting my arm around clients and letting them see that somebody was on their side."

Along with being an able and compassionate attorney, Balick shared Biden's political beliefs. He got Biden involved in a political organization called the Democratic Forum. The organization was working to reform the Democratic Party in Delaware. Its members believed that the state party was lagging behind the national party, especially on matters of civil rights and race relations. While the national party was becoming more progressive on those matters, Delaware Democrats were largely opposing school integration and open housing.

In February 1970, Biden's second son, Robert Hunter Biden, was born. Working two jobs, being a husband and father, and attending weekly meetings of the Democratic Forum was keeping Biden extremely busy. But, instead of being overwhelmed,

Biden was reveling in all that activity. He was actively and avidly pursuing the path that he had wanted to follow.

"I was practicing law that I believed in and I was getting involved in politics. I was right where I wanted to be." Biden's first run for political office came after a senior member of the Democratic Forum asked him to run for the New Castle County Council. At first, Biden was reluctant to run. The district was nearly 60 percent Republican, and he didn't have much knowledge about what the office entailed. He was also thinking about starting his own law firm. Those were two big negatives.

On the positive side, Biden was young (twenty-seven) and there were some heavily Democratic precincts in the district. Even if he lost, Biden would get some valuable, firsthand knowledge of what it takes to run a political campaign. If he won, the county council could be a springboard to future successes.

Before committing himself, Biden got Neilia's approval to run. Then, he recruited his sister, Valerie, to be his campaign manager. Biden knew that he wasn't going to win without getting a strong crossover vote from the Republicans. So he emphasized issues

Downtown Wilmington, Delaware

that were important to them. He courted their support by making door-to-door visits in the Republican strongholds.

"I knew how to talk to them [Republicans]. I understood that they valued good government and financial austerity and, most of all, the environment. I promised them to try to check the (land) developers and fight to keep open space."

In November 1970, Biden was elected to the New Castle County Council with a 2,000 vote margin. Biden's victory was a surprise to many political observers. He won in a district with a history of electing Republicans. Biden also did it during a time when Delaware Democrats weren't winning many elections.

After taking his seat on the county council, Biden quickly established a reputation for opposing corporations and the building industry. He didn't see him himself as being anti-business or anti-growth. Biden felt that environmental considerations and consequences had to be strongly considered.

"I became known as the guy who took on the builders and the big corporations. I was all for businesses creating jobs and wealth, but I thought that the companies that would profit owed

a fair accounting of the real costs. "Let Shell prove to us they won't ruin our environment, I'd say. 'If they can't prove it, we'll rezone them right out of here.'"

While serving on the county council, Biden was becoming a well-known figure to the movers and shakers in Delaware's Democratic Party. In 1971, the party leaders formed a twenty-five member Democratic Renewal Commission. The commission's objective was to modernize and revitalize the state's Democratic Party. Biden was the youngest member of the commission.

Among Biden's duties on the commission was working to find a strong candidate for the 1972 U.S. Senate race in Delaware. It was a difficult task because the nominee would be running against a very popular Republican incumbent. J. Caleb Boggs had previously served as governor of Delaware and had served in the House of Representatives before being elected to the Senate. Boggs was first elected to the House of Representatives when Biden was only three years old. Since then, he had never lost an election.

Biden and some other commission members asked former Delaware governor Bert Carvel to run. He turned them down. Then, they turned to Judge James M. Tunnell Jr., who had served as the associate justice of the Delaware Supreme Court. Tunnell also declined their offer. Every potential candidate they approached turned them down. The conventional wisdom was that Boggs was probably unbeatable.

Since no one seemed to want the nomination, the party leaders turned to Biden. Before saying yes, Biden thought of several reasons for saying no. He had additional family responsibilities after the birth of his third child, Naomi. Biden was also trying to build up a private law practice. And as a practical politician, he knew that Boggs would be very hard to beat.

Opposite page: Biden with his sons Hunter, left, and Beau. The photo was taken around 1972.

Still, Biden couldn't say no because he believed there was a chance that he could win. And if he did, he could work on the issues that mattered to him on a national instead of a county level. There was also the possibility that he might not get another chance to run for such a high office.

"How many other twenty-eight-year-olds ever get in the position to even consider such a move? As a senator I knew that I could have an effect on the issues that mattered to me: war and peace, the environment, crime, civil rights, women's rights."

Biden started seeking input from the party leaders. He found little or no resistance since no one else wanted to take on Boggs. Neilia encouraged him because she knew how passionate Biden was about politics. Biden finally decided that the potential rewards outweighed the present risks.

"Only a handful of people outside the family thought that I had a real shot to win, so I figured, even if I lost, people were going to say, 'That's a nice young guy. That's a serious young guy.' I couldn't see anything about the race that could hurt me. I was confident I could be a solid candidate. And I actually believed that I could win."

Biden ran a low-budget campaign in which several family members pitched in to help. His sister, Valerie, served as his campaign manager. Her husband served as the campaign's budget director. Biden's brother, Jimmy, was in charge of fund-raising and his mother organized coffee hours where Biden would meet and greet women voters at a supporter's home. To save money on postage Biden had a corps of teenage volunteers to hand deliver his campaign brochures.

Early in the campaign Biden freely acknowledged that he was a big underdog. But he kept insisting that if he connected with enough voters, that would change. "If I were a bookie, I'd give five-to-one odds right now that Boggs will be reelected, I'd tell them. But I wanted to let them know that I was running to win. If I can get to the people, I can beat Boggs."

Biden took a liberal stance on most issues. He called for an end to the Vietnam War and for a national health care system to protect families from being bankrupted by huge medical bills. Biden also took strong stands in favor of civil rights, voting rights, consumer protection, and environmental protection laws and increased funding for mass transit.

Biden was able to get his message out, but it looked like Delaware voters weren't very receptive to it. In early August, a statewide poll gave Boggs a 47 to 19 percent lead over Biden. But

Biden carries both of his sons, Beau, left, and Hunter, during an appearance at the Democratic State Convention in 1972. At center is his wife Neilia, and with them are Governor-elect Sherman W. Tribbitt and his wife, Jeanne.

the huge lead had made the Delaware Republicans complacent. They concentrated their resources on the race for governor. By early October, a poll showed that Biden had a two-point lead over Boggs.

But while Biden's campaign was gaining momentum and attracting more volunteers, it was running out of money. Ten days before the election, the radio stations threatened to quit running Biden's ads. They wanted to be paid in advance for all the future ads. Biden's campaign was spending $20,000 a week on the ads. By taking out a $20,000 loan, Biden kept his ads on the air until election day.

On election day, Biden pulled off a narrow upset. There were more than 230,000 votes cast and Biden won by 3,162 votes. At that time, Biden wasn't even old enough to serve as a U.S. senator. The constitution mandates that senators have to be thirty years old. Biden was about two weeks shy of his thirtieth birthday. His surprising election drew national attention. An article in *Newsweek* analyzed his surprising victory: "With three terms as congressman, two as governor and two more as senator, J. Caleb Boggs, sixty-three, seemed to enjoy the enduring confidence of Delaware voters. But the folksy GOP incumbent found himself hard-pressed by the unexpected Washington challenge of Joseph Biden, twenty-nine. The liberal Wilmington lawyer hammered away at the issues of environment, health care, mass transit and tax reform, and in a major upset squeaked through with 51 percent of the vote."

Biden and Neilia made an early exit from their election night victory party. When they got home, they talked about all the ways that their lives were going to change. A new residence, new schools for their boys, and if they'd need to get babysitters for their infant daughter.

Biden gave the microphone to his wife, Neilia, on election night, November 1972.

"Best of all, we talked about being a United States senator. I could actually do what we've been talking about all these months. We weren't just going to be a vote, we'd say; we were going to be a voice."

But, the elation and euphoria from his election triumph was abruptly ended by a grievous family tragedy a week before Christmas. It would leave Biden doubting his deep seated religious faith, pondering his political future, and even testing his will to live. "Get up," the two-word credo that had inspired him and shaped his life, now seemed to lose its meaning.

Chapter 3

Tragedy

On the morning of December 18, 1972, Biden was in Washington while Neilia was at their home in Wilmington. She stayed behind to do Christmas shopping and pick up a tree. Biden was in his Senate office with his sister, Valerie, when she got an unexpected phone call. Biden quickly noticed how pale her face was after the brief conversation. His instincts told him that something was dreadfully wrong.

Valerie told him: "There's been a slight accident." Then she reassured Biden that it wasn't anything to worry about, but they should return to Wilmington as soon as possible.

Biden knew that it was worse than she was letting on. He asked her: "She's dead, isn't she?" Valerie's silence confirmed his worst fears, but Biden kept telling himself that everything was going to be okay. He told himself that he was overreacting and that his imagination was running wild. But when he got to the hospital, he quit pretending.

Biden's brother, Jimmy, greeted them. When Biden saw Jimmy's face, he knew that the worst had happened. Neilia and his infant daughter, Naomi, had been killed instantly when a tractor-trailer crashed into their car. His two sons, Beau and Hunter, had survived, but they sustained serious injuries. For a time, the immense tragedy tested Biden's will to live, but he knew that he had to be there for his sons.

"Most of all I was numb, but there were moments when the pain cut through like a shard of broken glass. I began to understand how despair led people to just cash it in; how suicide wasn't just an option, but a rational option. But I'd look at Beau and Hunter asleep and wonder what new terrors their own dreams held, and wonder who would explain to my sons my being gone too. And I knew I had no choice but to fight to stay alive."

The tragic accident did much more than take away a wife and daughter. Politics, public service, and his religious faith had been the constants that had helped to give Biden's life meaning and purpose. Now, none of that seemed to matter to him anymore. Biden told Mike Mansfield, the senate majority leader, that he no longer wanted to be a senator.

"Delaware could always get another senator, I told people, but my boys couldn't get another father."

Biden's spirits were briefly lifted when he learned that his two sons would make full recoveries from their injuries. Yet, that wasn't enough to ease his anger and bitterness or to restore his faith in God.

"I didn't want to hear anything about a merciful God. No words, nor prayer, no sermon gave me ease. I felt that God had played a horrible trick on me, and I was angry. I found no comfort in the church."

While Biden was still dealing with his grief, anger, and his religious doubts, Senator Mansfield was constantly calling him. Mansfield simply refused to let Biden give up his seat in the Senate. He reminded him of how hard Neilia had worked to help him get elected. He told Biden that he owed it to Neilia and his sons to serve as a senator.

Mansfield's persistence paid off when Biden reluctantly agreed to serve six months before deciding if he wanted to serve the full six-year term. Biden took the oath of office in his son's hospital room. Instead of moving his family to Washington, Biden kept his house in Wilmington and commuted to work on Amtrak. It was a four-hour round trip, but it enabled him to spend every evening with his sons.

When Biden arrived in Washington, Mansfield, along with Democratic senators Ted Kennedy and Hubert Humphrey, did their best to make him feel welcome and needed. Still, Biden was unenthusiastic and apathetic about being a senator.

"I still wasn't sure that I wanted to be there. Some days I just wanted to be away from everything. . . . I had no interest in establishing personal relationships with the press, the staff, or my colleagues in Washington. My days were focused on when I could leave Congress and head back home."

When his sons were released from the hospital, Valerie and her husband, Bruce, moved into Biden's Wilmington home. She served as a substitute mother for the boys. Biden continued his

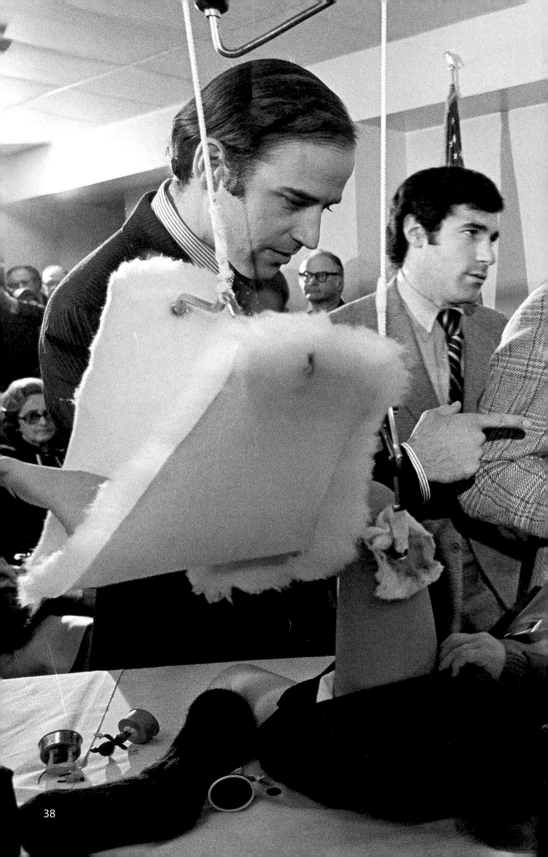

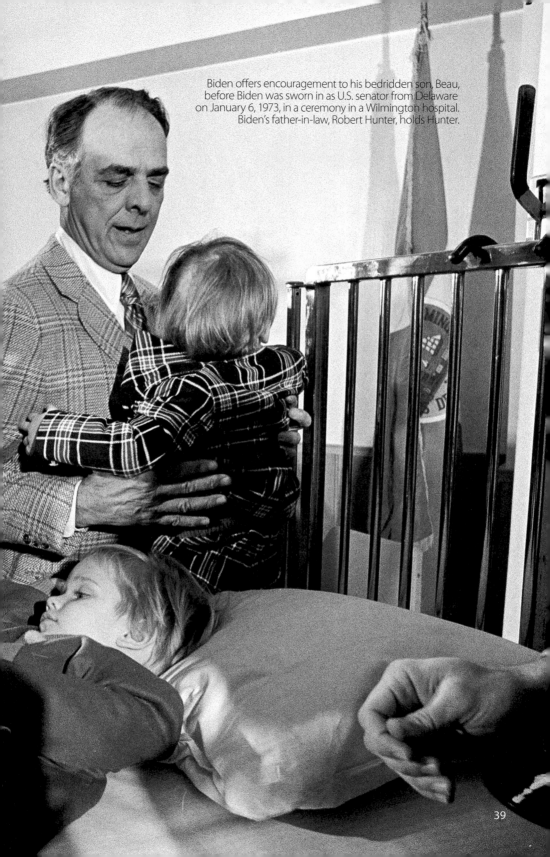

Biden offers encouragement to his bedridden son, Beau, before Biden was sworn in as U.S. senator from Delaware on January 6, 1973, in a ceremony in a Wilmington hospital. Biden's father-in-law, Robert Hunter, holds Hunter.

Biden with his two boys, Beau and Hunter

Amtrak commute so he could spend his evenings with his boys. The boys also had their dad's permission to call him anytime or go to Washington with him whenever they wanted.

Once Beau and Hunter adjusted to the big changes in their lives, Biden began to feel more like he belonged in the Senate. When his six-month trial run ended, he still was undecided about serving out his term. But, he was starting to enjoy some aspects of the job.

"I still wasn't sure that I was going to finish out my first term, but I liked that I could be focused, at least episodically, on my job."

During the 1974 congressional off-year elections, Biden made numerous speeches for his fellow Democrats. It was like being on the campaign trail again and it revitalized him. Amid all the speeches, handshaking, and traveling, Biden overcame his overwhelming grief. "Somewhere in the middle of all that running around I began to make my peace with God or with myself. Quite frankly, I just got tired of wallowing in grief. I started to think of my rage at God as an unbecoming form of egotism. What was more self-indulgent than to think that God had been busying himself with my particular circumstances?"

Biden took the healing process one step farther when he began dating. In March 1975, he saw Jill Jacobs for the first time. He became attracted to her when he saw photos of her in a series of ads. The ads were promoting the New Castle County Park System and they were being displayed at the Wilmington airport.

"She was blond and gorgeous," Biden recalled. "I remember thinking to myself, 'That's the kind of woman I'd like to meet.'"

Thanks to his brother, Frank, Biden did get to meet her. The same evening that he noticed Jill's photos, Frank gave him the phone number of a lady he thought Biden would like to meet.

He told Biden that he would like her because she wasn't interested in politics. But Biden didn't call her because he still thought that he wasn't ready to start dating.

The next day Biden changed his mind. Not knowing it was the model in the ads, Biden called the mystery lady. Her first response was to ask him how he got her phone number. Biden explained that he got her number from his brother. Then he quickly asked her if she could go out with him that evening.

Jill turned him down since she already had a date. Still, Biden persisted. He asked her if she could break it. Jill told him to call her back in an hour. One hour later, Biden called again and Jill told him that she was free. When Biden met her, he was a bit stunned to see that he was going out with the woman in the ads. "When I got to her door, there was the woman that I'd seen in the airport photographs . . . in person."

Their first date was dinner and a movie. Jill was exactly like Biden's brother had described her. She had no interest in politics and didn't ask Biden anything about his senatorial career. Biden found that refreshing. They talked about things like books, family, and friends. After one date, Biden was feeling like he could fall in love again.

"That night, for the first time since Neilia, I felt something like absolute attraction—and something like joy."

Jill Biden

Jill was in her last year of college and she found Biden to be vastly different than the other men she had been dating. He was older, more suave, and much better dressed than most of her other dates. "I had been dating guys in clogs and T-shirts," Jill recalled, "and he came to the door and he had on a sport coat and loafers, and I thought, God, this is never going to work, not in a million years. He was nine years older than I am!"

To her surprise, she found herself enjoying his company. When Biden took her home, he surprised Jill again by giving her a gentlemanly handshake instead of a good night kiss. Even though it was 1:00 a.m., Jill called her mother when she got home and told her: "Mom, I finally met a gentleman."

Biden and Jill went out two more times over the next two nights. All the while, Jill emphasized that she wasn't looking for a long-term relationship. She was only twenty-four, nine years younger that Biden. Jill had married young and was in the process of divorcing her husband. She was enjoying being single again, and she wasn't interested in becoming a politician's wife.

Biden wasn't discouraged. After having three dates in three nights, he was smitten. He called Jill again the same day that he returned to Washington. This time, he asked her not to date anyone else. Jill said okay, but she told Biden that she had a date the following weekend that she couldn't break. That was okay with Biden. He'd already decided that he could change her mind about not wanting a long-term relationship.

"I sure knew that wooing her was going to be difficult. But she'd said okay, and that was a start."

Biden's budding romance with Jill was making him more focused on his work as a senator. He was forging friendships with colleagues from both parties. Biden began speaking out on issues that he thought were vitally important to all Americans—such as drugs and crime. He argued that if America gave foreign aid to Turkey, then Turkey should shut down its illegal opium trade with the United States. On crime he still believed in trying to eliminate the root causes, but he also believed in dealing harshly with violent offenders.

"I was all for tackling poverty and unemployment and gaps in education . . . but it was equally important to lock up people when they committed violent crimes."

Biden was finding that for all of its pomp and power, the Senate had something in common with any other organization; there would be some members that you didn't like very well. In Biden's case it was Jesse Helms, a conservative Republican from North Carolina. After he heard Helms make a speech in the Senate, Biden shared his feelings with Mike Mansfield. He told Mansfield: "I can't believe guys like Helms. He's got no heart. . . ."

Before he could say anything else, Mansfield cut him off. He told Biden that everyone who served in the Senate had something good about them. Mansfield reminded Biden that the voters in North Carolina saw something good about Helms. Then he told Biden that his job was to look for the good in his colleagues instead of focusing on the bad.

Mansfield concluded by giving Biden some advice about engaging in political attacks. "And Joe, never attack another man's motive, because you don't know his motive."

Biden would later recall how sensible and important Mansfield's advice was. "There was nothing difficult about taking Mansfield's advice. In the Biden family, even as children, there had always been an assumption of good intentions. . . . We start with an assumption of goodwill toward one another. The same should hold true in the Senate family. It's probably the single most important piece of advice I got in my career."

While Biden was growing fonder of the Senate, he was also growing fonder of Jill. Even though she didn't care for politics, she reignited his passion for being in the political arena. Because of her, Biden was warming up to the idea of running for reelection. "She gave me back my life; she made me start to think that my family might be whole again. For the first time the Senate seemed fun. When I fell for Jill, I started to feel normal again, like I might be capable of running for a second term."

But if Biden was going to commit to reelection, he had to know if Jill was going to commit to him. Sometime in 1976, he asked her to marry him. Jill demurred by saying that she wasn't ready. According to Biden, over the next few months he proposed to her five more times. He always got the same disappointing response that she wasn't ready for another marriage.

In 1977, Biden gave her an ultimatum. His patience was exhausted and he was about to leave on a ten-day trip to South Africa. In a firm but loving way, he told her: "Look, I've waited long enough. I'm not going to wait any longer. Either you decide to marry me or that's it. . . . I'm too much in love with you to just be friends." During his ten days in South Africa, Biden was preoccupied with Jill. He had decided that

Mike Mansfield

if she finally said yes, he wouldn't run for reelection. When he got back from his trip, she gave him the news he'd yearned to hear. After Biden told her that he would leave the Senate to be with her, she told him that wasn't necessary. Sometime later, she explained why.

"If I denied you your dream," Jill said, "I would not be marrying the man that I fell in love with."

Jill probably didn't realize it then, but Biden's dream was a lot bigger than just serving another term in the Senate.

Chapter 4

First Defeat

O n June 17, 1977, Biden and Jill were wed by a Catholic
priest at a United Nations chapel. They had the wedding outside of Delaware to avoid publicity. Even
though the ceremony was for family only, they had around forty
guests there. After a brief honeymoon in New York City, Biden
returned to the Senate and Jill took on the duties and responsibilities of helping to raise two sons.

Biden continued his daily Amtrak commutes and on most
nights he was back in Wilmington to enjoy a late dinner with
Jill and the boys. Jill had to be the stay-at-home mom. She had
to be the cook, cleaner, and chauffeur while Biden was away.

Although she didn't care for politics, Jill took a supportive role in Biden's 1978 reelection bid.

Biden was in a difficult race because he had taken a stand that surprised and disappointed many of his liberal and African American supporters. He opposed the enforced busing of public school students to achieve racial balance in schools. Along with Delaware's other senator, Republican William Roth, he introduced a bill to restrict busing.

Biden had always prided himself in his strong commitment to civil rights and working to end discrimination in housing, employment, and education. Now, he was being accused of becoming a pawn of racists. He tried to explain that his opposition was largely based on his deep concern for the quality of the schools. But no matter what he said or did, it seemed like a lose-lose situation.

"Busing was a liberal train wreck and it was tearing people apart. The quality of the schools in and around Wilmington was already suffering, and they would never be the same. Teachers were going to be transferred without consultation to new school districts. In some instances, they would be forced to take a pay cut. . . . White parents were terrified that their children would be shipped into the toughest neighborhoods in Wilmington; black parents were terrified that their children would be the targets of violence in the suburban schools."

As election day neared, the busing issue became even more intense. Teachers went on strike in Delaware to protest the plan. That delayed the start of the school year. In late October, a ruling by the U.S. Supreme Court allowed the controversial busing plan to be implemented.

Although Biden had been running ahead in the polls, he wasn't feeling good about his chances of being reelected. The

1978 midterm elections were viewed as a referendum on the policies and popularity of President Jimmy Carter and his fellow Democrats. Carter, who had previously served as governor of Georgia, had won a narrow victory over the incumbent president, Gerald R. Ford, in 1976. For Biden and many other Democrats, a growing inflation rate was a cause for concern.

In October 1978, Carter instituted measures to fight inflation. During Carter's first eighteen months as president the inflation rate jumped from 7.2 percent to 10.8 percent. The unemployment rate during that time dropped from 8.1 percent to 5.7 percent. Still, more voters were concerned about inflation than unemployment. Republicans were making political inroads by hammering away at the issue of "double-digit inflation."

On election day, Biden found that his fears of losing were groundless. He defeated his Republican opponent, James H. Baxter, by more than 27,000 votes. But several of Biden's Democratic congressional colleagues didn't fare as well. The Democrats lost three seats in the Senate and fourteen in the House. Biden was happy to win, but he was even happier that the campaign was over.

"I think that election came down to trust. The people of Delaware believed that I was trying to do the right thing and I wasn't being partisan. By the numbers I won fairly easily—58 percent to 42—but it felt a lot closer than that. In fact, it felt more like an escape than a victory."

The Democratic losses in the 1978 midterm elections were a prelude to a Republican landslide in 1980. Biden had been the first elected official outside of Georgia to endorse Carter's presidential candidacy in 1976. In 1980, Biden was continuing to support Carter, but he knew that the Democrats were in trouble. The Republicans had nominated former California

Senator Joe Biden, center, is sworn in by Vice
President Walter Mondale, January 15, 1979, in Washington, D.C.
Biden's parents, Joseph R. Biden and Catherine Eugenia Biden, are on the left.

governor Ronald Reagan to run against Carter. Reagan was a
savvy campaigner who attacked Carter for runaway inflation
and his inability to free fifty-two Americans being held as hos-
tages in Iran.

Most pollsters and political pundits predicted a close election,
but Reagan won a stunning victory by carrying forty-four of the
fifty states. His convincing win also allowed Republicans to gain
control of the Senate and pick up thirty-two seats in the House.
After eight years in the Senate, Biden was no longer a member
of the majority party.

Four years later, Reagan was reelected by an even wider
margin. He carried forty-nine of fifty states while routing the
Democratic nominee, former Vice President Walter Mondale.
But even though Reagan carried Delaware by more than 50,000

votes, Biden was easily reelected to a third term in the Senate. He defeated his Republican opponent, John M. Burris, by more than 49,000 votes.

Throughout the Reagan presidency, Biden was a visible and vocal critic of the president. He opposed Reagan's attempts to reduce various benefits under the Social Security program. He vigorously, but unsuccessfully opposed Reagan's nomination of Edwin Meese as attorney general. Biden also opposed the confirmation of Associate Justice William Rehnquist as chief justice of the U.S. Supreme Court. In spite of Biden's strong opposition, Rehnquist was confirmed by a vote of 65-33.

In the 1986 midterm elections, the Democrats regained control of the Senate and Biden became the chairman of the Senate Judiciary Committee. Shortly after assuming the chairmanship, Biden found himself opposing another Reagan Supreme Court nominee. This time the nominee was so controversial, Biden was able to defeat him.

Robert H. Bork had a record of scholarship, public service, and strongly conservative views. Bork had served as both solicitor general and acting attorney general of the United States. He also had judicial experience from serving as a judge on the District of Columbia Circuit of the United States Court of Appeals. Bork's credentials as a legal scholar were bolstered by his service as a professor at the Yale Law School.

But from the moment Bork was nominated by President Ronald Reagan, pro-choice, civil rights, and women's rights groups strongly opposed Bork. The pro-choice groups claimed that Bork's stated belief that the U.S. Constitution didn't ensure a general "right to privacy" indicated that he would vote to overturn the Supreme Court's pro-choice *Roe v. Wade* decision.

The civil rights groups believed that Bork would vote to reverse earlier Supreme Court decisions that had favored them. The American Civil Liberties Union (ACLU) also opposed Bork's nomination. That was only the third time that the ACLU had opposed a Supreme Court nominee.

One of the most scathing attacks against Bork came from Massachusetts senator Ted Kennedy. Less than an hour after Bork's nomination was announced, Kennedy delivered a blistering attack on the new nominee. "Robert Bork's America is a land in which women would be forced into back-alley abortions, blacks

Ronald
Reagan

would sit at segregated lunch counters, rogue police would break down citizens' doors in midnight raids, schoolchildren could not be taught about evolution."

Biden had also stated his opposition to Bork shortly after his nomination. Still, he was credited with conducting the Senate hearings fairly. The hearings gave Bork a forum for explaining and defending his views. Biden was able to frame the discussion around the belief that the U.S. Constitution gives rights of liberty and privacy that aren't explicitly stated. That was a belief that Bork didn't share with Biden.

The Senate Judiciary Committee rejected Bork's nomination by a 9-5 vote. Despite the rejection, the nomination still moved on to the Senate. On October 23, 1987, the Senate rejected Bork's nomination by a 58-42 vote. Six Republican senators split with their party by voting against Bork. After the vote Bork's supporters maintained that his views had been misunderstood. His opponents said that he was rejected because Biden and other senators understood his views and believed that most

Ted Kennedy

Americans didn't share them. While Biden enjoyed his victory, he didn't gloat about it or savor it. He was smarting from having to withdraw from the race for the 1988 Democratic Party's presidential nomination.

In June 1987, Biden had announced his candidacy for the 1988 Democratic presidential nomination. He entered a crowded field that included his Senate colleagues, Al Gore of Tennessee and Paul Simon of Illinois. Congressmen Richard Gephardt of Missouri, Arizona governor Bruce Babbitt, Massachusetts governor Michael Dukakis, and the Reverend Jesse Jackson were also vying for the nomination.

While campaigning at the Iowa State Fair in August 1987, Biden gave a speech where he quoted a passage from a campaign ad used by Neil Kinnock, the leader of the British Labour Party. That was followed by further disclosures that he used unattributed quotes from Robert F. Kennedy and Hubert Humphrey in another speech. Shortly after that, yet another story appeared reporting that Biden had plagiarized an article from the *Fordham Law Review* article while he was in law school. In prior speeches Biden had remembered to credit Kinnock for the quote he used.

Maureen Dowd of the *New York Times* was the first journalist to report on Biden's unattributed use of the Kinnock quote. The story was also prominently reported in Iowa's largest newspaper, the *Des Moines Register.* It was later learned that aides from the Dukakis campaign had distributed a video of Biden quoting Kinnock without attribution. The video also showed Kinnock saying some of the same lines that Biden had used.

Biden fought back by calling a press conference to address the plagiarism charges. He had already explained that quoting Kinnock without attribution was an oversight and a big mistake. The quotes from Kennedy and Humphrey were from a speech writer who neglected to mention the source. Biden further explained that the law school plagiarism charge was because he hadn't been diligent in going to class and learning how to do citations.

But no amount of explanations and apologies could undo the past. The media had been unrelenting in questioning Biden's character and integrity. Biden couldn't find a single reporter to come to his defense. That was hugely disappointing, but Biden accepted that he was the one person responsible for the attacks.

"When I stop trying to explain to everybody and thought it through, the blame fell totally on me. Maybe the reporters traveling with me had seen me credit Kinnock over and over, but it was Biden who forgot to credit Kinnock at the State Fair Debate. I had been immature and skipped class and blown the Legal Methods paper. I was the one who thought it was good enough to just get by in law school."

Governor Dukakis said that he had no knowledge of staffers making and distributing the video. Dukakis fired his campaign manager, John Sasso, but that didn't help Biden's troubled campaign. In late September 1987, Biden announced that he was withdrawing from the race for the Democratic nomination.

In announcing his withdrawal, Biden looked and sounded more sad than bitter. He emphasized that he was reluctant to quit the race, but he hinted that he might seek the nomination at a later date. He also

Biden, center, points to a crowd as his train leaves, after he announced his candidacy for president, in June 1987. At right, Biden's son Beau carries daughter Ashley. Next to Biden is Jill and son Hunter.

Biden with Jill looking on holds a news conference announcing that he is withdrawing from the Democratic race for the presidential nomination.

referred to the ongoing Bork nomination hearings as a factor in his decision. Biden said that his first responsibility was "to keep the Supreme Court from moving in a direction that I believe to be truly harmful."

Then he expressed his displeasure at having to quit and alluded to his future plans. "Although it's awfully clear to me what choice I have to make, I have to tell you honestly, I do it with incredible reluctance and it makes me angry. . . . There will be other presidential campaigns and I'll be there, out front."

While campaigning for the presidential nomination, Biden had been suffering from persistent headaches. He may have assumed that they were job and campaign related. Between the plagiarism charges and the Bork confirmation hearings, Biden had been under a lot of stress. But he would learn that it was something much more than a headache, it was a life threatening illness.

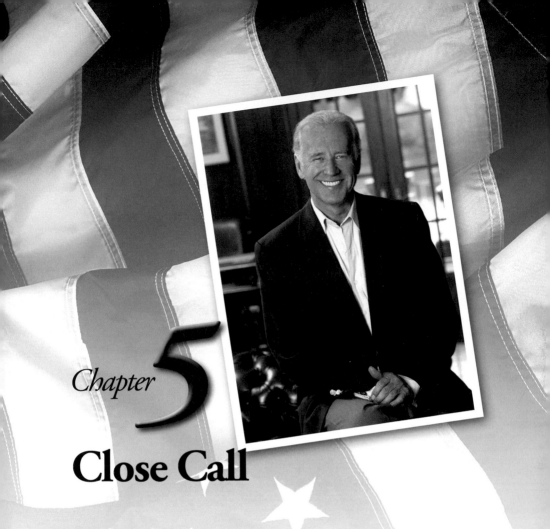

Chapter 5

Close Call

I n February 1988, Biden made a speech in Rochester, New York. He was elated by the warm reception he received. He returned to his hotel room and thought about ordering something to eat. But before he could order anything, he collapsed at the foot of his bed. Biden was unconscious for about the next five hours.

When he awakened, he couldn't remember where he was. Then, he felt some extremely intense pain. "Something like lightning flashing inside my head, a powerful electrical surge—and then a rip of pain like I'd never felt before."

With great effort, he crawled into bed and stayed there until his friend and traveling companion, Bob Cunningham, arrived. He helped Biden to get on a flight back to Wilmington. Cunningham and Biden's aide, Tommy Lewis, got Biden home from the airport. They asked Biden if he wanted to see a doctor, but he told them he'd be okay once he got home. Shortly after Biden got home, someone notified Jill that Biden seemed to be seriously ill. "She [Jill] didn't even ask me what I wanted to do. The next thing that I knew, we were on our way to St. Francis Hospital."

Biden underwent a spinal tap which, revealed that there was blood in his spinal fluid. That meant that an artery inside his head was leaking blood. More tests had to be done. The additional tests showed Biden had an aneurysm just below the base of his brain.

An aneurysm is a bulging blood vessel. It occurs when a spot in the blood vessel weakens and blood pressure forces the vessel to swell like an inflated balloon. Almost half of all ruptured aneurysms end up being fatal. Many other times, an aneurysm can cause a lifelong disability.

Biden's best chance of survival was to undergo a dangerous and delicate operation. Biden's brother, Jim, began calling to find a quickly available neurosurgeon who had performed the procedure. Jim found that their best chance was to send Biden to the Walter Reed Medical Center, outside of Washington, D.C.

Additional tests at Walter Reed showed that Biden was suffering from two aneurysms on the left and right sides of his brain. The aneurysm on the right side was the smaller of the two and less likely to immediately burst. It was decided that there would have to be two separate operations.

Opposite Page: Biden flanked by Jill and daughter Ashley meets with reporters after his release from Walter Reed Medical Center in May 1988.

61

The complex and difficult procedure is known as a microsurgical craniotomy. It requires the surgeon to open up the skull and lift the brain slightly so there's enough space to get to the aneurysm. Once the aneurysm is found, it's dissected and a small metal clip is attached to the artery to stop the bleeding. But, if anything goes wrong, the patient can be seriously impaired.

Biden was well aware of the risks, but he remained calm and put his faith in the surgeons, Dr. Eugene George and Dr. Neal Kassell. Once again, life had knocked Biden down. Biden understood that this time getting up was beyond his power. It was out of his hands. "It surprised me. But I had no real fear of dying. I'd long since accepted the fact that life's guarantees don't include a fair shake. And there was literally nothing that I could do to save myself."

In the final minutes before the operation, Biden talked to his two sons. He told them how proud he was of them. Biden added that he expected to be okay, but if something happened he wanted them to take care of their mother and sister. Then, he joked about the epitaph that he wanted on his tombstone.

After seven hours of surgery, Biden slowly regained consciousness. One of his first sensations was feeling Jill kiss him on his forehead. Biden still wasn't sure if he was awake or in a haze from the anesthesia. He asked Jill if he was alive. He was elated to hear her reassure him that he'd survived the delicate and risky surgery.

But the elation soon wore off when he was bedridden for ten long days. Most of the pain was gone, but the boredom and immobility were unrelenting. Biden had to depend on nurses to bathe him and brush his teeth. "I wasn't sure that I had what it took to keep going. . . . the early days of recovery were unremittingly difficult. . . . in my few waking hours the only way to fill the time was to lie and stare at the graphs measuring my systems. . . . All I could do was stare at the screens, knowing that if one of those lines or bar graphs went flat, I was a goner."

Biden was released from Walter Reed with the understanding that he would return for an operation on the second aneurysm when he got his strength back. Biden was confident that he'd make a full and speedy recovery. But during his convalescence, he suffered yet another serious setback. One morning, he felt an intense pain in his abdomen and chest. He was too weak to get out of bed.

Biden was taken to a local hospital. Doctors there discovered that he had a blood clot lodged in one of his lungs. That wasn't uncommon for someone who had been bedridden for long periods of time. But the doctors were concerned that there might be other clots. If there were, a

Walter Reed Medical Center

clot could break free and travel to Biden's heart or lungs. That could be fatal.

Biden returned to Walter Reed. For the next week and a half surgeons, specialists, and nurses tended to him. Biden underwent yet another operation where a titanium filter was installed in an artery around the middle of his thorax. The filter would catch any breakaway blood clots and prevent them from traveling on to his heart or lungs. The doctors also put him on an anticlotting drug to clean his arteries and break down blood clots.

In May 1988, Biden had an operation for the second aneurysm. Dr. George used a microscope to pinpoint the location of the aneurysm. Then, he pinched the aneurysm with a clip that brought the walls of the artery together. The procedure took four-and-a-half hours. Following the operation, Peter Esker, a spokesman for the Walter Reed Medical Center, announced that Biden was awake, resting comfortably, and talking to members of his family.

Biden's convalescence was slow. It took a few months before he could resume all of his Senate duties. After getting cleared by his doctors, Biden returned to Washington in September 1988. By that time, both parties had chosen their presidential nominees. The Democrats chose Massachusetts governor Mike Dukakis and the Republicans picked Vice President George H. W. Bush.

After Dukakis took an early lead in the polls, the Bush campaign steadily gained momentum. Bush easily won by getting 54 percent of the popular vote and carrying forty states. Still, the Democrats were able to maintain control of the House and Senate. That enabled Biden to stay on as chairman of the Senate Judiciary Committee.

In 1990, Biden was reelected to a fourth term in the Senate. He defeated his Republican opponent, M. Jane Brady, by more than 48,000 votes. The race attracted little attention outside of Delaware. Brady ran on an anti-incumbents platform and she proposed limiting members of Congress to only two terms.

Shortly after his reelection, Biden conducted confirmation hearings on another controversial Supreme Court nominee. In July 1991 President George H. W. Bush nominated Judge Clarence Thomas to succeed Justice Thurgood Marshall. Initially, it looked like Thomas would have no trouble being confirmed. Marshall had been the first African American to serve on the U.S. Supreme Court. If Thomas were confirmed, he would become the second.

But Thomas had opposed abortion rights and affirmative action programs. Civil rights groups such as the Urban League and the National Association for the Advancement of Colored People (NAACP) were quick to oppose his nomination. Women's groups like the National Organization of Women (NOW) were worried that Thomas would vote against continuing legal abortions.

Despite their opposition, the confirmation hearings were relatively quiet and uneventful. Thomas sidestepped questions on legal abortion by saying that he hadn't formed an opinion on the issue. Still, the Judiciary Committee didn't approve his nomination. The vote was seven for confirmation and seven against it. The nomination moved on to the Senate without the Judiciary Committee's approval.

Thomas's nomination became even more controversial after information was leaked saying that Thomas had sexually harassed one of his staff members when he served as the chairman of the Equal Employment Opportunity Commission (EEOC). Anita Hill, a law professor at the University of Oklahoma, claimed that Thomas sexually harassed her during their tenure at the EEOC.

Clarence Thomas

Hill claimed that Thomas had engaged in discussions of pornographic films and sexual acts after she had refused to date him.

Biden came under attack by fellow Democrats and women's groups for failing to use Hill's accusations to block Thomas's nomination. Biden had shared her accusations with other members of the Judiciary Committee. Since Hill had initially been reluctant to testify against Thomas, Biden thought it was unfair to use her charges against him.

Ultimately it became a case of she-said, he-said. It was Hill's word against Thomas's. A small majority of senators found Thomas to be more credible. He was confirmed by a vote of 52-48. That was the closest confirmation vote for a Supreme Court justice in more than one hundred years.

Biden's conduct at the confirmation hearings disappointed and even angered various feminist and women's organizations, but his authoring and fight for the Violence Against Women Act (VAWA) helped him to regain their favor. He first introduced the act in 1991, but it wasn't signed into law until 1994.

A major reason for the delay was the strong opposition of Chief Justice William H. Rehnquist. The act had a civil rights component that allowed women victimized by violence to sue their attackers for damages in federal court. Rehnquist claimed that it would overburden the docket of federal courts and that matters of violence against women were best left to the jurisdiction of state courts. He further claimed that it would encourage women to make false claims so they could receive larger alimony payments.

Biden responded to Rehnquist's claims by saying: "Now we have got a Chief Justice who, I respectfully suggest, does not know what he's talking about when he criticizes this legislation."

U.S. Capitol, Washington, D.C.

The results of the 1992 presidential and congressional elections helped to give the VAWA the support to get it enacted. Some political writers heralded 1991 as the "Year of the Woman" because a record number of women ran for public office and won. In the Senate elections, eleven women ran and five of them won.

In the presidential election, President George H. W. Bush lost his bid for reelection to the Democratic nominee, Arkansas governor Bill Clinton. Along with Clinton's election, the Democrats retained control of both houses of Congress.

When the VAWA passed, it had become part of a larger bill entitled the Violent Crime Control and Law Enforcement Act (VCCLEA). The VCCLEA is the largest crime bill in American history. Because of Biden's high-profile support, it also became known as the "Biden Crime Bill." The bill authorized the appropriation of more than $9 billion for prison funding and nearly another $6 billion for funding crime prevention programs. It also increased penalties for drug trafficking, the smuggling of illegal aliens, and gang-related crimes.

While Biden was taking great satisfaction in the passage of the landmark crime bill, he was becoming increasingly concerned and vocal about violence in what was once the Federal Republic of Yugoslavia. From 1945 to 1980 the country had been ruled by a wily Communist dictator named Josip Broz Tito. But about a decade after Tito's death the once united nation began coming apart. In 1991 and 1992, four of the six republics that made up the federal republic declared their independence.

In the Republic of Serbia a ruthless tyrant named Slobodan Milosevic seized control. Milosevic soon expanded his sphere of influence by stripping the republics of Kosovo and Vojvodina of their autonomy. By suppressing dissent, financing militia groups, and encouraging Serbs to rid Serbian-held areas of all the non-

Serbian residents, Milosevic earned the nickname "butcher of the Balkans."

The violence and killing that Milosevic condoned led Biden to become one of the Senate's most outspoken members in denouncing the brutal dictator. As Serbs continued to torture, kill, and imprison Muslims in the province of Bosnia, Biden repeatedly called for the U.S. to intervene. After seeing that most of his Senate colleagues were unwilling to take action, Biden expressed his frustration in a Senate speech.

"In the twenty-three years that I have been here, there is not another issue that has upset me, angered me, frustrated me, and occasionally made me feel a sense of shame about what the West, what the democratic powers of the world are allowing to happen . . . we have stood by—we the world—and watched in the twilight moments of the twentieth century, something that no one thought would ever happen again in Europe."

After Biden introduced a resolution authorizing President Bill Clinton to intervene, the North Atlantic Treaty Organization (NATO) began an air strike campaign that led to Milosevic's surrender. In 2002, Milosevic went to trial before an International Criminal Tribunal on charges of war crimes. But, he died in his prison cell before the trial ended.

On September 11, 2001, the United States endured the worst terrorist attack in its history. Two hijacked jet airliners crashed into and toppled the twin towers of the World Trade Center in New York City. A third hijacked airliner crashed into the Pentagon, the home office of the U.S. Department of Defense. The series of attacks killed approximately 3,000 people.

When the attacks occurred, Biden was making his usual Amtrak commute to Washington. He arrived in Washington shortly after the third plane hit the Pentagon. When he looked

Flames and smoke pour from a building at the Pentagon on September 11, 2001. Inset: A helicopter flies over the burning Pentagon.

Smoke, flames, and debris erupt from one of the World Trade Center Towers as a plane strikes it.

at the sky beyond the Capitol dome, Biden saw a cloud of hazy brown smoke.

It was quickly determined that terrorist leader Osama Bin Laden and his al-Qaeda cohorts were behind the attacks. It was also a well known fact that the Taliban, which ruled Afghanistan, was supporting al-Qaeda and possibly sheltering Bin Laden and other al-Qaeda leaders. President Bush called for the Taliban rulers to turn Bin Laden over to the U.S. government and to close terrorist training camps in Afghanistan.

When the Taliban refused, the U.S. launched an invasion of Afghanistan. It was a move that Biden wholeheartedly supported.

"George W. Bush had a reputation for impatience, but in the weeks immediately following the 9/11 attacks, I saw a president who was rational, thoughtful, resolute, and balanced. I saw a president who went to the American people and to the entire international commu-

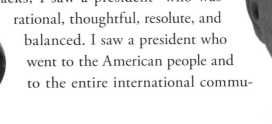

George W. Bush

5

nity and made a compelling case for action in Afghanistan," Biden said.

The invasion was able to quickly and easily topple the Taliban, but Biden's support wavered when American aid to rebuild the country was slow in coming. The rift between Biden and the Bush administration became deeper when administration officials began linking Iraqi leader Saddam Hussein to the terrorist attacks. Still, Biden voted in favor of the 2002 resolution authorizing the war against Iraq.

But after the invasion failed to find any weapons of mass destruction and an Iraqi insurgency led to mounting American casualties, Biden became an outspoken critic of the war. In 2004, a scandal broke over the mistreatment of Iraqi prisoners of war at an American run prison in Abu Ghraib. Biden responded to the scandal by saying President Bush should fire his secretary of defense, Donald Rumsfeld.

Although he wasn't seeking the Democratic presidential nomination in 2004, Biden was optimistic that his party could regain the presidency. If that happened, there was a very real chance that Biden could play a major role in a new administration.

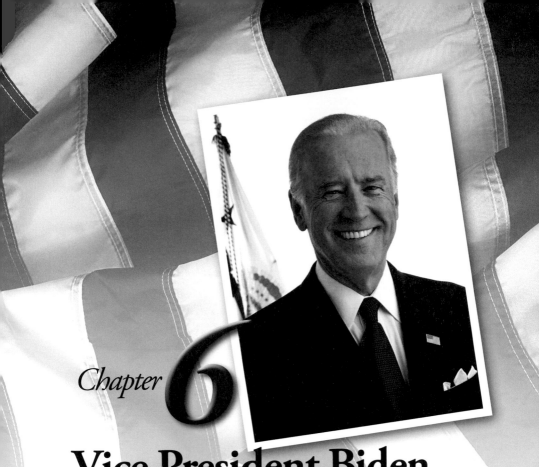

Chapter *6*

Vice President Biden

I n 2004, President George W. Bush was running for reelection against the Democratic nominee, Senator John Kerry of Massachusetts. Kerry had served in the Senate since 1985 and was a decorated veteran of the Vietnam War. Biden and many other Democrats were optimistic that Kerry would be elected. The Bush administration's conduct of the Iraq War made the Republicans look vulnerable.

There were mounting American casualties as the war looked like it would indefinitely continue. A major justification for going to war was that Iraq had weapons of mass destruction (WMDs). After months of searching, no WMDs had been found. Also,

in May 2004, reports had surfaced that American soldiers had abused Iraqi prisoners of war (POWs) at the Abu Ghraib prison in Iraq.

Yet, the Republicans were able to turn the tables and put Kerry on the defensive by saying that he had misrepresented his war record and that he couldn't be trusted. The top strategists in Kerry's campaign advised him against rebutting the charges. They believed that rebutting them would make them more credible.

In November 2004, Bush was reelected by a margin of around 3 million votes. He carried 31-of-50 states for a 286-251 margin in the Electoral College. Biden was taken aback by the loss. He had firmly believed that Kerry would win. The unexpected loss got him thinking about making another run for the presidency. "Had John Kerry won the election it would have closed off the question of my running for president of the United States. And I think it upset her [his wife Jill] that the question was back on the table. I was pretty sure that I knew where she stood. Jill had only one thing in mind. Her instinct was to protect me and to protect the family—and she understood that my running for the Democratic presidential nomination in 2008 meant the entire Biden family would have to make big sacrifices."

During his second term, Bush's approval ratings steadily dropped. Opposition to the Iraq War continued to grow. The 2006 congressional elections were being viewed as a referendum on the Bush administration's domestic and foreign policies. It's common for the party in power to lose seats in a midterm election. But, the results surprised many political writers and commentators.

The Democrats exceeded their expectations by gaining six seats in the Senate and thirty-one in the House. For the first time in twelve years, they would control both houses of Congress. Less than a month after the new democratic-controlled Congress was sworn in, Biden became a candidate for the 2008 democratic presidential nomination.

When Biden announced his candidacy, Senators Hillary Clinton and Barack Obama had already entered the race. At that time, Clinton was viewed as the front-runner for the nomination with Obama being a close second. Biden acknowledged that when he appeared on ABC-TV's *Good Morning America.* He admitted that Clinton was the front-runner and he called Obama a "real star."

In spite of his lengthy Senate tenure, Biden didn't have name recognition with the voters, which Clinton and Obama enjoyed. Political writer Greg Giroux summed up the difficulties Biden faced by writing: "The 64-year-old Biden, despite his 34 years in the Senate and frequent media appearances, lacks the celebrity factor of the Democrats currently topping presidential polls of Democratic voters: Senators Hillary Rodham Clinton of New York and Barack Obama of Illinois whose combined total of just more than eight years of Senate service measures to less than a quarter of Biden's own tenure."

Another perceived handicap was Biden's vote in October 2002 authorizing President George W. Bush to invade Iraq. Senator Clinton had also voted for the measure. Obama was able to run as an antiwar candidate because the vote occurred before he was in the Senate. Biden later called his vote a mistake, but to many antiwar Democratic activists, it seemed like a case of politically expedient hindsight.

Still, there was no question that Biden was the most experienced of the three candidates. He emphasized that in announcing his candidacy.

Senator Barack Obama announces his candidacy for president of the United States in front of thousands at the Old State Capitol in Springfield, Illinois, on February 10, 2007.

81

"I'm running for president because I think that, with a lot of help, I can stem the tide of this slide and restore America's leadership in the world and change our priorities," he said during a conference call with reporters. "I will argue that my experience and my track record—both on the foreign and domestic side— put me in a position to be able to do that."

Biden did have the advantage of having some readily available campaign funds. He was also up for reelection to the Senate in 2008. Federal campaign finance laws allow a mem-

Democratic presidential hopeful Biden gets advice from New Hampshire senator Sylvia Larson.

Biden speaks during a town hall meeting about Iraq at Coker College in Hartsville, South Carolina, in March 2007.

ber of Congress to transfer money from a House or Senate campaign to a presidential campaign account. Biden had more than $3 million in his Senate campaign account when he entered the presidential race.

While $3 million sounds like a lot of money, it wasn't close to what he would need to run an effective, competitive presidential race. That became apparent after the Iowa Caucus in January 2008. Eight Democratic candidates were on the ballot in Iowa. Biden finished in fifth place with only about 1 percent of the vote. That was less than half of what some recent polls had indicated.

The caucus decided which candidates Iowa's delegates to the Democratic and Republican

National Conventions would support. Obama won the votes of sixteen delegates. North Carolina senator John Edwards finished second and picked up fifteen delegates. Clinton was third with thirteen delegates.

All three of the leading candidates greatly outspent Biden on TV ads. Biden spent $1.8 million in Iowa on TV ads. Obama

spent five times as much ($9 million) and Clinton spent four times as much ($7.2 million) as Biden. It was obvious that Biden didn't have the funds to compete. The day after the caucus, he withdrew from the race.

When he ended his campaign, Biden did his best to be positive and upbeat. He told his loyal supporters: "There is nothing

Biden, left, listens as Barack Obama responds to a question during the first democratic presidential primary debate of the 2008 election, on April 26, 2007. At right is Hillary Rodham Clinton.

Biden speaks at a caucus rally in Des Moines, Iowa, in January 2008 after abandoning his bid for the Democratic presidential nomination.

sad about tonight. We are so incredibly proud of you all. So many of you have sacrificed for me, and I am so indebted to you. I feel no regret."

After withdrawing from the race, Biden held off on endorsing any of the other Democratic candidates. Eventually, the field was narrowed down to just Clinton and Obama. Then in June 2008, Clinton announced that she was suspending her campaign and endorsing Obama.

With Obama assured of the presidential nomination, the next business for his campaign was the selection of a running mate. There was speculation that he would choose Clinton, but in late August 2008, Obama announced that Biden would be his running mate.

By that time, Arizona senator John McCain had cinched the Republican presidential nomination. Members of the McCain campaign were quick to bring up some of the negative things that Biden had said about Obama.

Before dropping out of the race, Biden had said that Obama was "not yet ready" to be president. Later, during his unsuccessful campaign, Biden was forced to apologize to Obama for calling him "the first mainstream African-American who is articulate and bright and clean and a nice looking guy." The characterization was widely regarded as being racially insensitive. Obama graciously accepted the apology by reminding voters of Biden's commitment to civil rights throughout his political career.

"I have absolutely no doubt about what is in his heart and the commitment he has made to racial equality," Obama said. "So I will provide some testimony, as they say in church."

On August 27, 2008, Biden gave his acceptance speech at the Democratic National Convention in Denver. In his speech he hammered away at McCain's consistent support of the Bush-Cheney administration and how the Obama-Biden ticket would bring "the change we need." Those would be two of the recurring themes during his vice-presidential campaign.

While attesting to McCain's courage and heroism as a POW (prisoner of war) during the Vietnam War, Biden said that 95 percent of the time, McCain's Senate votes sided with the current administration. He attacked McCain's voting record by repeatedly saying "that's not change; that's more of the same."

Three days after Biden's acceptance speech, he learned who his Republican opponent would be. Senator McCain made a surprising choice by announcing that Governor Sarah Palin of Alaska would be his running mate. Prior to the announcement, it was believed that McCain had narrowed his choices to Massachusetts governor Mitt Romney, Minnesota governor Tim Pawlenty, and Connecticut senator Joe Lieberman.

Some political observers saw McCain's pick as an attempt to woo the women that had supported Hillary Clinton. Palin was

Biden hugs Obama after Obama took the stage in a surprise visit to the Democratic National Convention after Biden delivered his vice presidential nomination acceptance speech.

little known outside of Alaska. She had been elected governor in 2006 after serving as the mayor of Wasilla, Alaska.

Palin became the first woman to be nominated by the Republicans for vice president and the second woman to run for that office on a major party ticket. In 1984, Congresswoman Geraldine Ferraro had been the Democrats' nominee for vice president.

Clinton congratulated Palin for her "historic nomination," but quickly added that the policies of the McCain-Palin ticket "would take the country in the wrong direction." Obama campaign spokesperson Adrianne March was much harsher in her criticism of the Republican ticket. She attacked Palin's lack of foreign policy experience while echoing the time for a change theme of the Obama campaign.

"Today, John McCain put the former mayor of a town of 9,000 with zero foreign policy experience a heartbeat away from the presidency," Bill Burton, Barack Obama's campaign spokesman, said. "Gov. Palin shares John McCain's commitment to overturning *Roe v. Wade*, the agenda of Big Oil and continuing George Bush's failed economic policies. That's not the change we need; it's just more of the same."

In the next few weeks both Biden and Palin made some notable and newsworthy gaffes while campaigning. In an interview with Katie Couric on the *CBS Evening News,* Biden said: "When the stock market crashed, Franklin D. Roosevelt got on television and didn't just talk about the, you know, the princes of greed. He said, 'Look, here's what happened.'"

But when the stock market crashed in 1929, Herbert Hoover, not Franklin D. Roosevelt, was the president. At that time, Roosevelt was serving as governor of New York. Also, at that time, television was not how the president communicated with a mass audience. Radio was the major medium of electronic mass communications.

When answering a third grade student's question on what the vice president does Palin said: "A vice president has a really great job because not only are they there to support the president's agenda, they're there like a team member, the teammate to the president. But also, they're in charge of the United States Senate, so if they want to they can really get in there with the senators and make a lot of good policy changes . . . ."

The only constitutionally prescribed duties of the vice president are to preside over the Senate and to cast the deciding vote when there's a tie vote. Usually, the vice president doesn't spend much time presiding over the Senate. The Senate's pro tempore or another senator from the majority party does the presiding.

Maria Comella, a spokeswoman for Palin, explained what appeared to be a lack of knowledge about the position by saying: "Governor Palin was responding to a third grader's inquiry. She was explaining in terms a third-grader could understand that the vice-president is also the president of the U.S. Senate."

The campaign trail gaffes did a lot to pique interest in the upcoming vice-presidential debate. Democratic strategists were worried that Biden would say something that he'd later regret. Their concerns were magnified because he would be debating a woman. Political writer Mark Halperin explained the dilemma by noting: "Biden is in particular danger of saying something perceived as condescending or sexist to Palin."

Campaign strategists prepared Biden for the debate by using Michigan governor Jennifer Granholm as a stand-in for Palin. Reportedly, Biden also sought advice from female Senate colleagues Barbara Boxer, Dianne Feinstein, and Clinton.

The debate was held in St. Louis, Missouri, in early October 2008. Most observers agreed that there was no clear-cut winner. The general consensus was that both candidates met or exceeded expectations. Palin came off as being somewhat knowledgeable on the wide range of issues that were discussed. Biden didn't make any gaffes or act like he was being condescending to his opponent.

In their closing statements both candidates repeated the themes that they had emphasized throughout the campaign. Palin avoided mentioning the Bush-Cheney administration and referred to the 1981-1989 presidency of Republican Ronald Reagan. Biden once again referred to the need for "fundamental change."

Four weeks later Biden ended his campaign by making stops in Missouri, Ohio, and Pennsylvania. Ohio was considered to be a vitally important swing state. In 2004, Ohio's twenty electoral votes had given George W. Bush his winning margin over John Kerry in the Electoral College. At a campaign stop in Copley Township, Ohio, Biden delivered a scathing attack against the McCain-Palin campaign.

"They made a decision that the only way to get to the highest office was to take the lowest road you can take. They've been calling Barack Obama every single name in the book. This time [today], they will have to call him the forty-fourth president of the United States of America."

The Obama-Biden ticket had maintained a consistent lead in the polls throughout the race. Still, Biden refused to predict a victory. But *New York Times* reporter John M. Broder noted how Biden had become more confident and accessible to him and other reporters.

"You can see the confidence in Mr. Biden's smile and his new accessibility to the reporters who have accompanied him for two months. He spoke to them for 20 minutes on his plane, the first time that he has done so since early September."

Despite the confidence that he was showing, Biden wasn't taking any chances. Just in case the McCain-Palin ticket won, Biden was also running for reelection to the Senate. It was an election he easily won, but he was able to move up to an even higher office.

On Tuesday, November 4, 2008, the Obama-Biden ticket exceeded most expectations with a resounding victory. They won nearly 53 percent of the popular vote and carried twenty-eight of the states for an electoral vote margin of 363-175. The ticket's popularity carried over into the congressional elections. The Democrats picked up six seats in the Senate and eighteen in the House. For the first time in fourteen years, the Democrats would be in control of the White House and both houses of Congress.

But the Democrats barely had time to celebrate before Biden's penchant for gaffes would reemerge. One day before the inauguration Biden and Jill appeared as guests on *The Oprah Winfrey Show*. During the show, Jill claimed that Obama had offered Biden his choice of two positions—secretary of state or vice president. Biden responded by turning to Jill with his finger to his lips and going: "Shhh!"

Only three hours after the show aired Biden's spokeswoman, Elizabeth Alexander, was placed in the embarrassing position of denying Jill's claim. In a prepared statement, Alexander said: "To be clear, President-elect Obama offered Vice-President-elect Biden one job only—to be his running mate, and the vice-president-elect was thrilled to accept the offer."

Less than a week later Biden made a second heavily reported gaffe at a swearing-in ceremony for White House staffers.

President Barack Obama gives his inaugural address from the west steps of the U.S. Capitol on January 20, 2009. Inset: The official invitation to the inauguration ceremony.

The Presidential Inaugural Committee
requests the honor of your presence
to attend and participate
in the
Inauguration of

Barack H. Obama
as President of the United States of America

and

Joseph R. Biden, Jr.
as Vice President of the United States of America
on Tuesday, the twentieth of January
two thousand and nine
in the City of Washington

During President Obama's swearing in Chief Justice John Roberts flubbed the words to the presidential oath of office. During the ceremony, Biden joked about reciting the oath of office by saying: "My memory is not as good as Justice Roberts'." The flippant remark brought on a chorus of groans from the staffers and a sternly disapproving look from President Obama. It also brought on attacks from some Republicans.

Republican strategist Patrick Dorinson attacked Biden by declaring: "He's an embarrassment. Biden's reputation is going to suffer because people are going to realize that he's not that sharp, that he thinks that he's going to be this big shot."

Phil Trounstine, a democratic strategist, came to Biden's defense by saying Biden's tendency to speak in haste wasn't a problem. Trounstine also mentioned how Biden's predecessor, Vice President Cheney, had injured a friend in a hunting accident. "I don't think it's a problem," Trounstine said. "And if the Republicans want to make an issue out of it, they better remember: This guy hasn't shot anybody in the face yet . . . and I don't think that he will."

After the controversy over the gaffes subsided, Biden settled into his new position. By nearly all accounts, he's become actively engaged in promoting and pushing the programs of the new administration. Political writer Kenneth T. Walsh noted that Biden has taken on four major roles as vice president.

"Biden's role is fourfold: confidant to the president on a wide range of policy issues, especially foreign affairs; public surrogate to sell the administration's agenda; congressional lobbyist; and advocate for the middle class."

President Obama, a former high school basketball player, compares Biden's role to a basketball player "who does a bunch of things that don't show up in the stat sheet." Obama added that his vice president "gets that extra rebound, takes the charge, makes that extra pass."

It looks like Biden has been content with the role of being the unheralded team player in the Obama administration. As long as he continues to enjoy free access to the president, Biden will likely accept the vice-presidency as the capstone to a lengthy and remarkable political career. If Biden and President Obama are reelected in 2012, then Biden would be seventy-four years old when he leaves the vice-presidency. At that age, it seems unlikely that Biden would make another run for the presidency.

But whatever he decides, whatever fate awaits him, or whatever life gives him, as long as he can, Biden will keep following his father's advice and continue to get up.

Jill and Joe Biden with Barack and Michelle Obama

Timeline

1942
Born in Scranton, Pennsylvania, on November 20.

1953
Moves to Claymont, Delaware, with family.

1957
Attends Archmere Academy, a Catholic prep school.

1965
Graduates from the University of Delaware with a double major in history and political science; enrolls in Syracuse University law school.

1966
Marries Neilia Hunter, his college sweetheart.

1968
Graduates from Syracuse University Law School and takes job as a public defender.

1969
Son Beau born.

1970
Second son, Hunter, born; elected to the New Castle County City Council.

1971
Daughter Naomi Christina born.

1972
Wife Neilia and daughter killed in a car crash, and sons injured; wins first Senate election.

1973
Sworn in as senator beside sons' hospital bed.

1977
Marries his second wife, Jill Tracy Jacobs.

1978
Wins second term as senator.

1981
Daughter Ashley born.

1984
Reelected to a third term in the U.S. Senate.

1987
Announces candidacy for Democratic presidential nomination; withdraws.

1988
Diagnosed with two cranial aneurysms; undergoes successful surgery.

1990
Reelected to a fourth term in the U.S. Senate.

1996
Reelected to fifth term in the U.S. Senate.

2002
Reelected to a sixth term in the U.S. Senate.

2007
Declares his candidacy for the Democratic presidential nomination.

2008
Withdraws from presidential race after a poor showing in the Iowa Caucus; chosen by Democratic presidential nominee Barack Obama to be his running mate.

2009
Inaugurated as the forty-seventh vice president of the United States.

Sources

Chapter One: Get Up!

p. 11, "Get up . . . in the doing," Joe Biden, *Promises to Keep* (New York: Random House, 2007), xxii.

p. 12, "It wasn't always bad . . ." Ibid., 3.

p. 12, "As much as I lacked . . . " William Dovark, "Joseph R. Biden," *Current Biography*, March 2009, 3.

p. 13, "I prayed that I would . . ." Biden, *Promises to Keep*, 20.

p. 15, "Uncle Boo-Boo had . . ." Ibid., 21.

p. 15, "I beat the stutter . . ." Ibid., 23.

p. 16, "Joe was the kind of guy . . ." Charles Moritz, ed., *Current Biography Yearbook 1987* (New York: H. W. Wilson Company, 1987), 43.

p. 16, "In the first semester . . ." Biden, *Promises to Keep*, 27.

p. 17, "We see dozens . . ." Ibid., 28.

p. 18, "When she turned toward me . . ." Ibid.

p. 18, "I felt my heart go . . ." Ibid., 29.

p. 18, "I could feel myself sweating . . . " Ibid., 30.

p. 19, "You know we're going . . ." Ibid., 31.

p. 19, "I think so . . ." Ibid.

p. 19, "I had plenty of time . . ." Ibid., 33.

p. 20, "The deans and professors . . ." Ibid., 36.

p. 22, "His daughter was marrying . . ." Ibid., 37.

Chapter Two: Young Senator

p. 24, "I couldn't tell them . . ." Biden, *Promises to Keep*, 41.

p. 24, "The plaintiff . . ." Ibid., 42.

p. 24-25, "Being a public defender . . ." Ibid., 46.

p. 25, "I learned how to be . . ." Ibid., 47.

p. 26, "I was practicing law . . ." Ibid., 48.

p. 27, "I know how to . . ." Ibid., 50.

p. 27-28, "I became known as . . ." Ibid., 51.

p. 30, "How many other . . ." Ibid., 58.

p. 30, "Only a handful of . . ." Ibid., 59.

p. 30-31, "If I were a bookie . . ." Ibid., 61.

p. 32, "With three terms as . . ." *Newsweek*, November 13, 1972, 36.

p. 34, "Best of all, we talked . . ." Biden, *Promises to Keep*, 75.

Chapter Three: Tragedy

p. 35, "There's been a slight accident . . ." Biden, *Promises to Keep*, 79.

p. 36, "She's dead, isn't she . . ." Ibid.

p. 36, "Most of all . . ." Ibid., 80.

p. 36, "Delaware could always get . . ." Ibid.

p. 37, "I didn't want to hear . . ." Ibid., 81.

p. 37, "I still wasn't sure . . . " Ibid., 86.

p. 41, "I still wasn't sure that I was going to finish . . ." Ibid., 92.

p. 41, "Somewhere in the middle . . ." Ibid., 96.

p. 41, "She was blond . . ." Ibid., 100.

p. 42, ". . . when I got to her door . . ." Ibid.

p. 42, "That night, for the first time . . ." Ibid., 101.

p. 44, "I had been dating . . ." Jonathan Van Meter, "All The Vice-President's Women," *Vogue*, November 2008, 306.

p. 44, "Mom, I finally met . . ." Ibid.

p. 44, "I sure knew that . . ." Biden, *Promises to Keep*, 102.

p. 45, "I was all for . . ." Ibid., 106.

p. 45, "I can't believe . . ." Ibid., 110.

p. 45, "And Joe, never attack . . ." Ibid.

p. 45, "There was nothing difficult . . ." Ibid., 111.

p. 46, "She gave me back my life . . ." Ibid., 113.

p. 46, "Look, I've waited long enough . . ." Ibid., 115.

p. 47, "If I denied you . . ." Ibid., 116.

Chapter Four: First Defeat

p. 49, "Busing was a liberal . . ." Biden, *Promises to Keep*, 125.

p. 50, "I think that election . . ." Ibid., 128.

p. 53, "Robert Bork's America . . ." Ibid., 169.

p. 56, "When I stopped trying . . ." Ibid., 203.

p. 56, "to keep the Supreme Court . . ." E. J. Dionne Jr. "Biden Withdraws Bid for President in Wake of Furor," *New York Times*, September 24, 1987.

p. 56,58, "Although it's awfully clear . . ." Ibid.

Chapter Five: Close Call

p. 59,   ". . . something like lightning . . ." Biden,
          Promises to Keep, 218.

p. 60,   "she [Jill] didn't even stop . . ." Ibid.

p. 62,   "It surprised me," Ibid., 222.

p. 62-63, ". . . I wasn't sure that . . ." Ibid., 225.

p. 67,   "Now we have got . . ." Ibid., 246.

p. 71,   "In the twenty-three years . . ." Ibid., 283-284.

p. 75,   "George W. Bush had . . ." Ibid., 309.

Chapter Six: Vice President Biden

p. 78,   "Had John Kerry . . ." Biden, *Promises to Keep*, 355-356.

p. 79,   "real star . . ." Greg Giroux, "Delaware Sen. Joseph R. Biden Jr.
          Wednesday officially launched his well-expected candidacy
          for the 2008 Democratic presidential nomination,"
          CQPolitics.com, January 31, 2007, http://www.CQPolitics.com.

p. 79,   "The 64-year-old Biden…" Ibid.

p. 82,   "I'm running for president . . ." Ibid.

p. 85-86, "There is nothing sad . . ." Shailagh Murray, "Biden, Dodd
          Withdraw From Race," *Washington Post*, January 4, 2008.

p. 87,   "not yet ready . . ." Adam Nagourney and Jeff Zeleny, "Obama
          Chooses Biden as Running Mate," *New York Times*,
          August 23, 2008.

p. 87,   "the first mainstream African-American . . ." Ibid.

p. 87,   "I have absolutely no doubt . . ." Walter Shapiro, "Could be
          Biden Time," Salon.com, http://www.salon.com/news/
          feature/2008/07/02/biden_as_vp/print.html.

p. 87,   "the change we need . . ." "Transcript: Joe Biden's Acceptance
          Speech," http://ww.npr.org/templates/story
          story/php?storyID=94048033.

p. 87,   "that's not change . . ." Ibid.

p. 90,   "would take the country in the . . ." Ibid.

p. 90,   "Today John McCain put . . ." Ibid.

p. 90,   "When the stock market . . ." "In gaffe Biden said FDR led
          when market crashed," http://www.nowpublic.com/world/
          gaffe-biden-said-fdr-led-when-market-crashed.

p. 91,   "A vice president has a . . ." Brian Montopoli, "Would Palin
          Be 'In Charge' of the Senate?," http://www.cbsnews.com/
          blogs/2008/10/22/politics/horserace/entry4539032.shtm.

p. 91,   "Governor Palin was responding . . ." Ibid.

p. 91,   "Biden is in particular danger . . ." Mark Halperin, "Biden's Debate Challenge: Keeping His Mouth Shut," *Time*, October 2, 2008.

p. 94,   "They made a decision . . ." Stephanie Warsmith, "Biden makes final whirlwind stop in Ohio race," *Akron Beacon Journal*, November 4, 2008.

p. 94-95, "You can see the confidence . . ." John M. Broder, "Election Eve: Biden's Final Bouts," *New York Times*, November 3, 2008.

p. 95,   "To be clear . . ." "Was Biden offered choice of posts?," *Houston Chronicle*, January 20, 2009.

p. 98,   "My memory is not . . ." Carla Marinucci, "Can Biden learn to zip his lip?," *San Francisco Chronicle*, January 23, 2009.

p. 98,   "He's an embarrassment . . ." Ibid.

p. 98,   "I don't think it's a . . ." Ibid.

p. 98,   "Biden's role is fourfold . . ." Kenneth T. Walsh, "A Key Adviser and Confidant," *U.S. News & World Report*, June 1, 2009.

p. 98,   "who does a bunch of things . . ." Mark Leibovich, "Not a team player, but a valuable one," *Sarasota* (Fl.) *Herald-Tribune*, March 29, 2009.

Bibliography

Baker, Peter. "Biden Outlines Plan to Do More With Less Power." *New York Times*, January 15, 2009.

Biographiq. *Joseph Biden-From Scranton to Washington.* Filiquarian Publishing, LLC, 2008.

Biden, Joe. *Promises to Keep.* New York: Random House, 2007.

"Biden limbers up for office with scathing Cheney attack." (London) *Independent*, January 16, 2009.

"Biden Resting After Surgery for Second Brain Aneurysm." *New York Times*, May 4, 1988.

Broder, John M. "Biden's Record on Race Is Scuffed by 3 Episodes." *New York Times*, September 17, 2008.

"Election Eve: Biden's Final Bouts." *New York Times*, November 3, 2008.

Draper, Robert. "Joe Biden Can't Shut Up." *Gentleman's Quarterly,* March 2006.

Dvorak, William. "Joseph R. Biden." Current Biography, March 2009.

Feller, Ben. "Inauguration a culminating moment for Biden." *Baltimore Sun*, January 20, 2009.

Flintoff, Corey. "Biden, Palin Trade Jabs On Economy, War, Energy." ww.npr.org/templates/story/story.php?storyId=95284523.

Fouhy, Beth. "Honest Partner; Longtime senator moves into a supporting role as second in command." *St. Louis Post-Dispatch*, January 20, 2009.

Greenhouse, Linda. "Bork's Nomination Is Rejected, 58-42; Reagan 'Saddened'" *New York Times*, October 24, 1987.

Giroux, Greg. "Biden Announces Candidacy for 2008 Presidential Election." *New York Times*, January 31, 2007.

Halperin, Mark. "Biden's Debate Challenge: Keeping His Mouth Shut." *Time*, October 2, 2008.

Hellerman, Caleb. "Democratic VP nominee Biden releases medical records." http://www.cnn.com/2008/HEALTH/10/20/biden/health/ index.html.

Hill, Anita. *Speaking Truth to Power.* New York: Doubleday, 1997.

Koszczuk, Jackie, and H. Amy Stern, eds. *CQ's Politics in America 2006.* Washington, D.C.: CQ Press, 2005.

Lee, Carol. "Rove: Biden a 'blowhard' and 'liar.'" http://www.politico.com/news/stories/0409/21103.html.

Leibovich, Mark. "Not a team player, but a valuable one." *Sarasota* (Fl.) *Herald-Tribune*, March 29, 2009.

Libit, Daniel. "Joe Biden's Other Female Foe."
    www.christineodonnell08.com/2008/10/joe-bidens-other-
    female-foe.html.
Marinucci, Carla. "Can Biden learn to zip his lip?"
    San Francisco Chronicle, January 23, 2009.
"McCain taps Alaska Gov. Palin as vice president pick."
    http://www.cnn.com/2008/POLITICS/08/29/palin.republican.
    vp.candidate.
Moritz, Charles, ed. *Current Biography Yearbook*. New York: H. W.
    Wilson Co., 1987.
Murray, Shailagh. "Biden, Dodd Withdraw From Race."
    Washington Post, January 4, 2008.
Nagourney, Adam, and Jeff Zeleny. "Obama Chooses
    Biden as Running Mate." *New York Times*, August 24, 2008.
Navarrette, Ruben. "He's the guy running with Obama."
    Indianapolis Star, September 22, 2008.
Shapiro, Walter. "Could be Biden Time."
    http://www.salon.com/news/feature/2008/07/02/biden_as_vp/
    print.html.
Thomas, Clarence. *My Grandfather's Son*. New York:
    Harper, 2007.
The Undecided Voter's Guide to the Next President. New
    York: Harper Perennial, 2007.
Warsmith, Stephanie. "Biden makes final Ohio stop in
    whirlwind race." *Akron Beacon Journal*, November 3, 2008.
Walsh, Kenneth T. "A Key Adviser and Confidant." *U.S.
    News & World Report*, June 1, 2009.
"Was Biden Offered Choice of Posts?" *Houston Chronicle*,
    January 20, 2009.

Web sites

http://www.facebook.com/joebiden?_fb_noscript=1
Joe Biden's Facebook page.

http://www.ontheissues.org/Joe_Biden.htm
Learn where Joe Biden stands on a variety of issues at this Web site.

http://www. topics.nytimes.com/ top/ reference/ timestopics/ people/ b/ joseph_r_jr_biden/ index.html?inline=nyt-per
Find the latest news articles on Vice President Joe Biden on this site, as well as archived articles, photos, and videos.

http://www.esquire.com/features/joe-biden-biography-0209
Esquire magazine writer John H. Richardson provides a lengthy, insightful profile of Vice President Joe Biden in an article titled "Joe Biden, Advisor in Chief."

Index

Photo Credits

2: United States Federal Government/Andrew Cutraro/ White House photographer

8-9: Alamy/Colin Young-Wolff

10: AP Photo/Matt Rourke

11: Courtesy Archmere Academy

13: Courtesy Archmere Academy

14: Courtesy Archmere Academy

20-21: Andre Jenny/Alamy

23: AP Photo

26-27: Courtesy Tim Kiser (http://en.wikipedia.org/wiki/ File:Wilmington_Delaware_ skyline.jpg)

29: AP Photo

31: Associated Press

33: Associated Press

35: AP Photo/Bill Ingraham

38-39: AP Photo

40: Courtesy Archmere Academy

43: United States Federal Government/Ralph Alswang/ White House photographer

46: United States Congress

48: Associated Press

51: Associated Press

53: Executive Office of the President of the United States

54: United States Navy

56-57: AP Photo/George Widman

58: AP Photo/Ron Edmonds

59: United States Congress

61: AP Photo/Adelle Starr

63: Alamy/ Philip Scalia

66: United States Federal Government

68-69: Private Collection.

72-73: AP Photo/Will Morris; inset photo: AP Photo/Tom Horan

74: AP Photo/Chao Soi Cheong

75: United States Coast Guard

77: United States Federal Government/Andrew Cutraro/ White House photographer

80-81: AP Photo/Brian Kersey

82-83: AP Photo/Jim Cole

83: Top photo: AP Photo/Mary Ann Chastain

84-85: AP Photo/ J. Scott Applewhite

86: AP Photo/Jeff Chiu

88-89: AP Photo/Stephan Savoia

92-93: AP Photo/Don Emmert

96-97: AP Photo/Senior Master Sgt. Thomas Meneguin, Department of Defense/ US Air Force

99: Associated Press/Pat Jarrett/ *News Leader*

101: AP Photo/Gerald Herbert

Book cover and interior design by Derrick Carroll of DC Designs.